Table of Contents

Wildlife in the City

By Jean Bennett

Dominie Press, Inc.

Publisher: Raymond Yuen
Project Editor: John S. F. Graham
Editor: Bob Rowland
Designer: Greg DiGenti

Published by:

℗ Dominie Press, Inc.

1949 Kellogg Avenue
Carlsbad, California 92008 USA

www.dominie.com

1-800-232-4570

Paperback ISBN 0-7685-1842-3
Printed in Singapore by PH Productions Pte Ltd
1 2 3 4 5 6 PH 05 04 03

Chapter One
Small and Speedy

Most people hurry through city streets and take no notice of the wildlife all around them. It's amazing how many creatures live among the buildings and sidewalks.

Nature has some wonderful surprises

for anyone who stops to look. Our homes, schools, and streets are teeming with creatures that can survive wherever there is water and food.

Flies are common insects that zoom in on food or any smelly garbage that is lying around. A fly has taste buds on many parts of its body, including its feet.

Some insects have large eyes that are made up of hundreds of tiny parts. They can see in many different directions at once. That's why a fly always seems to know when someone is about to swat it.

Butterflies are insects that go through many changes to become the beautiful winged creatures we are familiar with.

A butterfly lays tiny eggs on a plant. A caterpillar hatches from an egg. The caterpillar eats the plant until it is full.

A caterpillar (top) and swallowtail butterfly

Then the caterpillar covers itself in a case, called a chrysalis, that it spins from its own silk.

Changes to the caterpillar take place inside the chrysalis. When it is ready, it cracks the chrysalis and emerges as a butterfly.

The "3 + 3 rule" is an easy way to identify insects. An insect has three pairs of legs and three parts to its body:

1. The head, with two feelers.

2. The chest (thorax), which carries the wings and legs

3. The abdomen, the lower body of the insect.

Moths go through life-cycle changes much like butterflies do. Most moths fly at night and are attracted to streetlights and brightly lit windows. Moths often have dark colors, so they're not easily seen in the shadows.

Insects have two feelers on their head, called antennae. Antennae allow an insect to find its way around and smell food. The mouths of many insects are shaped to stab and suck their food like a straw.

Wasps are attracted to sweet drinks and food. They are commonly found around garbage cans. Different kinds of wasps build their nests on walls, in attics, or in the ground. Like bees, wasps have the warning colors of yellow and black. Many have a nasty sting!

Cockroaches have been around for millions of years. Some kinds of cockroaches don't like light and only scurry around at night. They live in warm, dark places, like under refrigerators or in wood piles and loose bark. Cockroaches eat food scraps and other garbage.

Many small creatures have no bones or spines, which are also called backbones. Some have a hard shell to protect their soft bodies. Creatures without backbones are called invertebrates.

Beetles are everywhere. There are many different kinds of beetles, and they come in a variety of sizes and colors. Often they're so small we don't notice them. They usually have four wings—two hard wings form a protective covering

A rhinoceros beetle

over two softer wings that are used for flying.

Ants are hard workers. Look for small piles of dirt in cracks on sidewalks. These are made by ants digging their nest. An ant nest is a small underground city where every ant has work to do. The ants come and go in a constant stream, like cars on a freeway. They swarm around dropped food, especially sweet food. Some ants eat seeds and bugs.

Chapter Two
Wriggly and Wily

S_piders_ are great hunters. They catch insects that we sometimes think are pests. Spiders are not insects—they have eight legs and only two body parts. Many spiders weave sticky webs to catch their prey. Some spiders do not make webs,

Some spiders live in underground tunnels. Others are easy to see in webs in the corners of rooms or outside on buildings. Trees and bushes are home to many different kinds of spiders.

however. They hunt for insects and pounce on them like cats. Spiders belong to a group called arachnids, which also includes mites and scorpions.

An orb weaver spider

A giant desert centipede

Centipedes and millipedes are long and thin, with lots of legs. Centipedes live in damp basements, under houses, and outside. They feed on small insects and spiders.

Millipedes live outdoors and help to recycle waste by eating rotting plants. They are larger than centipedes. Sometimes they wander into basements and buildings. Some people keep them as pets!

Centi- means one hundred, and *milli-* means one thousand. Centipedes and millipedes don't really have exactly one hundred or one thousand legs, but they do have a lot.

Centipedes can have anywhere from 30 to 350 legs, depending on the species. One species of millipede has over 700 legs. Millipedes hatch with only a few legs and grow more as they get older!

Earthworms are busy creatures. They gobble up decayed plants and waste, which is cleansed as it passes through their bodies to enrich the soil. They burrow through dirt, making tunnels that let air and rain into the ground. Look for little piles of soil where the worms have been working.

A common lizard

Lizards are cold-blooded creatures
that love to lie in the sun on stones or
cling to walls. As they grow, they shed
their old skin and replace it with a new
skin that has grown underneath. They
hunt insects and spiders, and can move
very fast, especially when they're chased.
If a lizard is caught by its tail, the tail
snaps off to help the lizard escape. Then
it grows a new tail.

Snails creep along paths and gardens, leaving a slimy trail. Their lower body spreads out like a skirt and is called a *muscular foot*. This foot is very strong and can hold on to things much bigger than the snail itself.

A freshwater snail

Mice like to live in the walls of buildings and scamper around at night looking for food scraps. They share food with their family, sleep together, and keep themselves clean. They have a very high squeak, which can be heard far away by other mice.

Rats make nests for their babies from paper and dried grass. Their sharp teeth can chew through wood and plastic. They live in ditches, drains, ceilings, and under buildings. They eat garbage, insects, and other small animals. Rats can carry diseases to humans.

Chapter Three
Noisy Creatures

Although pet *crows* can learn to talk, they mostly cry a harsh *caw caw*. The inky-black birds eat insects, fruit, and small animals. They also help the environment by cleaning up the remains of dead animals.

Magpies, part of the crow family, are just as rowdy as their crow cousins. These black-and-white birds are clever thieves—they steal eggs and shiny objects. They build nests thickened with mud.

When *starlings* sing, they copy the songs of other birds. They flock together and nest in buildings and trees. Glossy and dark-colored, they waddle around like important business executives. Starlings

A starling

eat insects, but they can become pests when they attack fruit trees.

All birds have feathers, wings, and beaks. The bones of most birds are hollow. This makes them lighter for flight.

Bats have high-pitched squeaks that help them find their way. Their cries echo back from objects so they can judge distance. Bats hang upside down in high, dark places like old buildings, hollow trees, or caves. They fly at night and mostly eat insects or fruit.

Bats have poor eyesight, which is why people often say someone is "as blind as a bat." They use sound instead of sight to find their way around in the dark.

The hoot of an *owl* at night can sound frightening. Owls have excellent hearing,

A barred owl

and they see well in the dark. They hunt mice and other small animals. Their hooked claws grip their prey tightly.

Dogs are noisy! They bark, yelp, whine, growl, and howl. Often they're making a fuss to protect their space, or to warn their owners about strangers. They hear sounds people can't hear, which makes them good guard dogs. A good sense of smell helps them hunt and track.

Cats purr, hiss, growl, and meow. Some cats are domesticated — they live with humans for food and comfort. Others are really wild animals. They

A cat

prowl city streets and hunt birds, mice, and insects. Cats can climb easily, using their hooked claws, and their whiskers help them measure narrow spaces so they won't get stuck. They have excellent hearing, and they see well at night.

Male **crickets** chirp loudly by rubbing their wings together. Some crickets live indoors, where they eat food scraps and can lay their eggs in warm places. Others are outdoor insects that eat seeds and plants and lay their eggs in the soil.

There are many insects and animals living in the city. Some of these creatures act as a clean-up crew by recycling wastes. Others help to keep the city free of pests that carry disease and illness.

Some creatures, such as fleas and mosquitoes, are harmful to people. But many creatures are beneficial to us.

> Fleas are parasites that live on some animals, such as cats and dogs. These tiny, biting insects suck the blood of their hosts, making them itch and scratch.

Birds and lizards, for example, feed on many of the creatures that we view as pests. We need to take care not to hurt the creatures that benefit people. The best way we can do this is not to damage the places where they live.